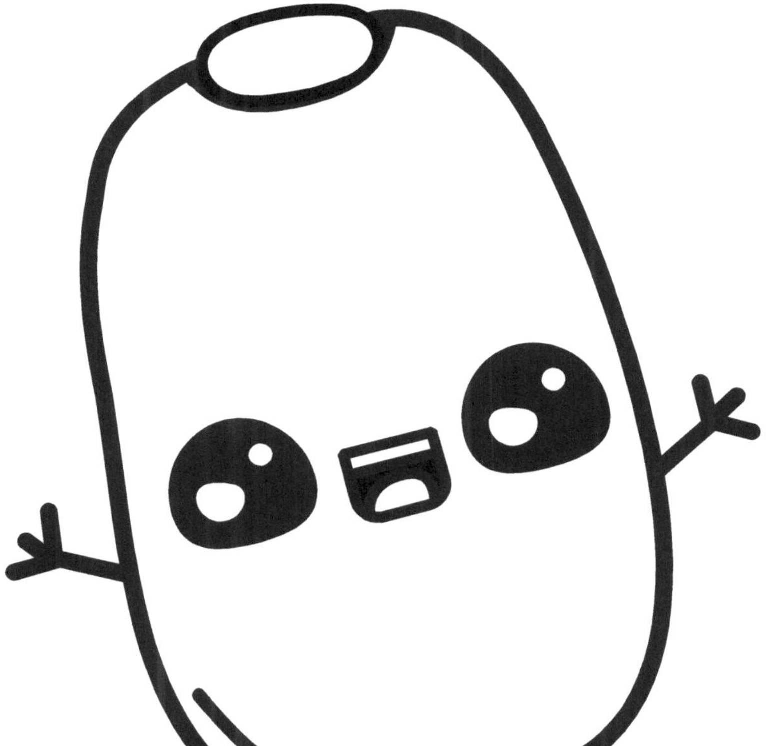

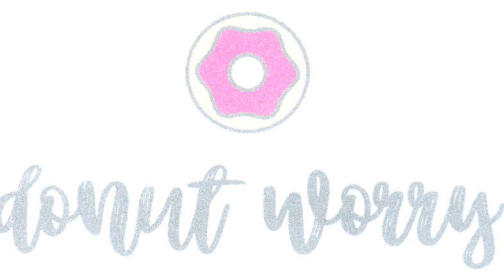

donut worry

THIS PAGE
INTENTIONALLY
LEFT BLANK
(FOR MARKER USERS)

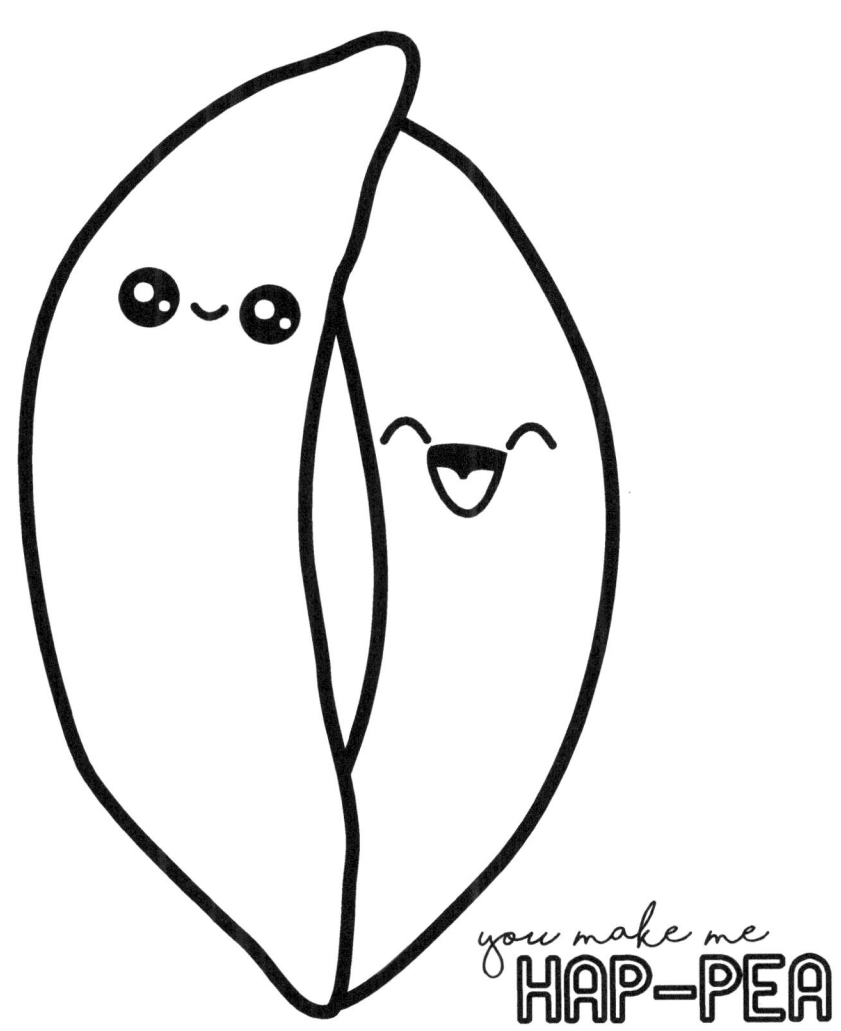

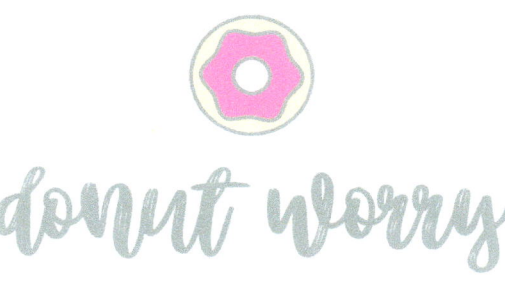

donut worry

THIS PAGE
INTENTIONALLY
LEFT BLANK
(FOR MARKER USERS)

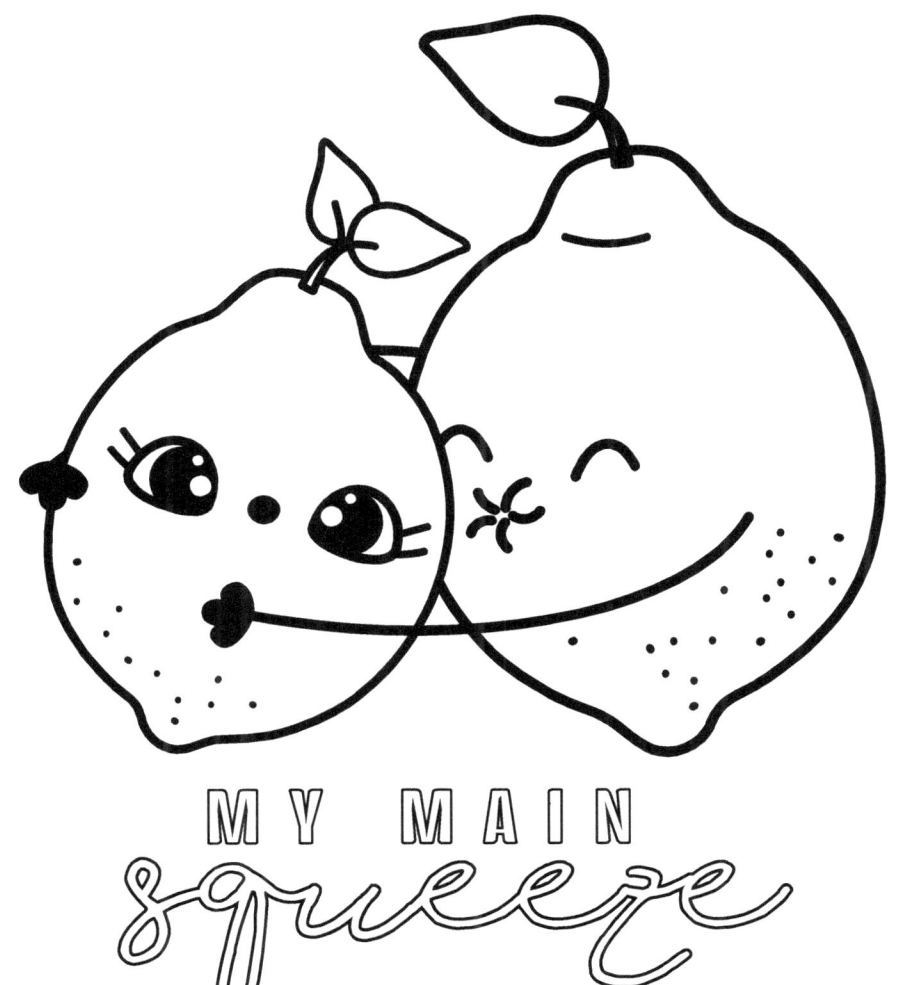

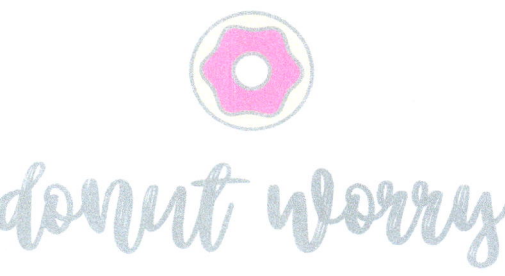

donut worry

THIS PAGE
INTENTIONALLY
LEFT BLANK
(FOR MARKER USERS)

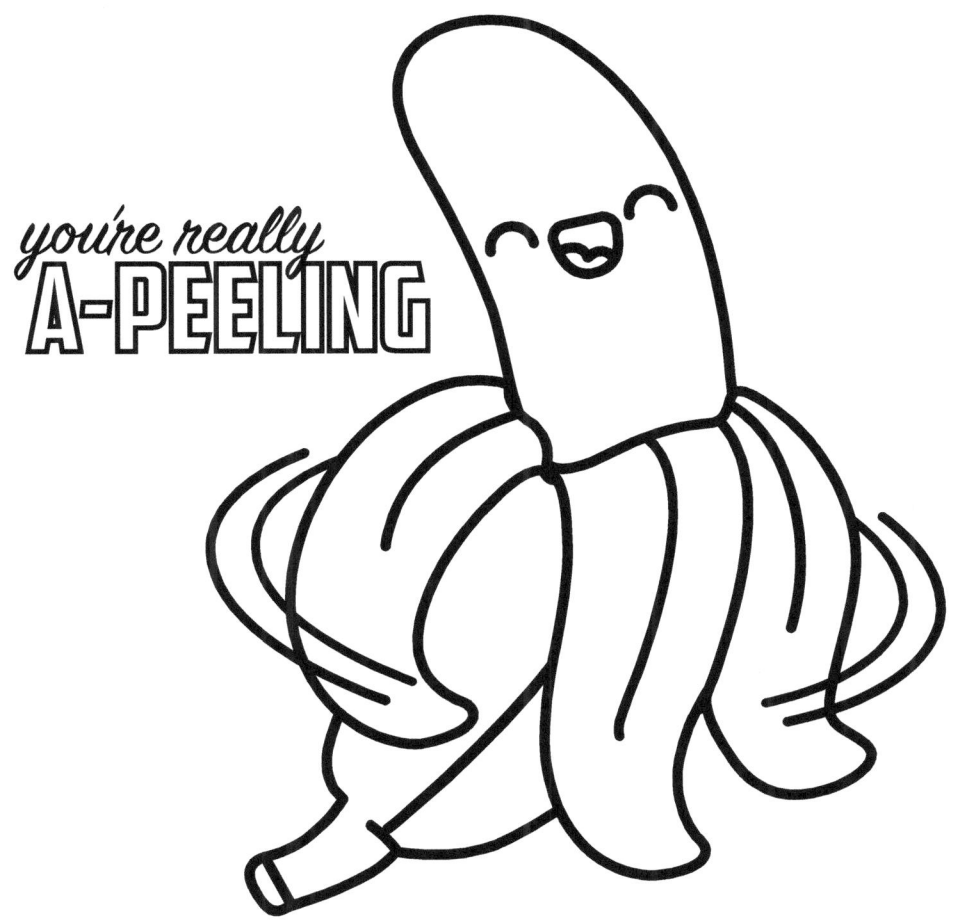

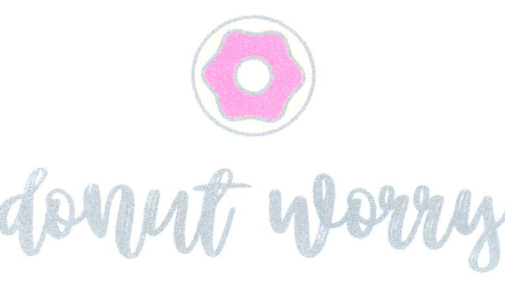

donut worry

THIS PAGE
INTENTIONALLY
LEFT BLANK
(FOR MARKER USERS)

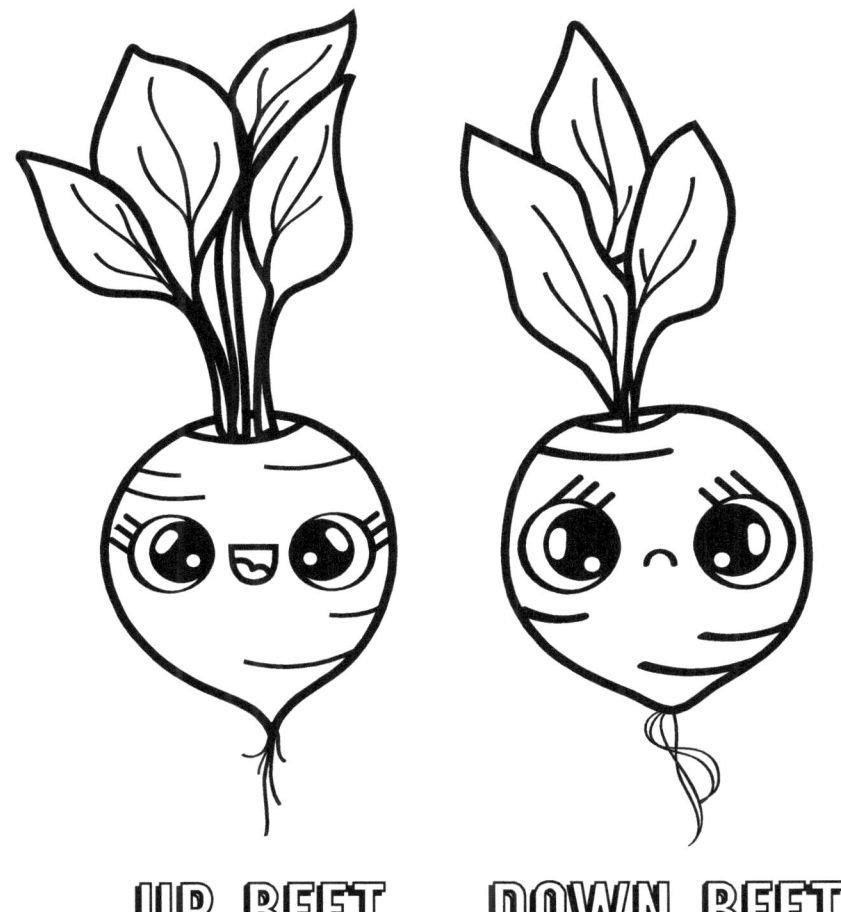

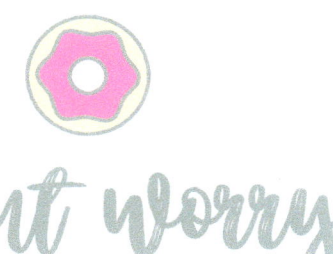

donut worry

THIS PAGE
INTENTIONALLY
LEFT BLANK
(FOR MARKER USERS)

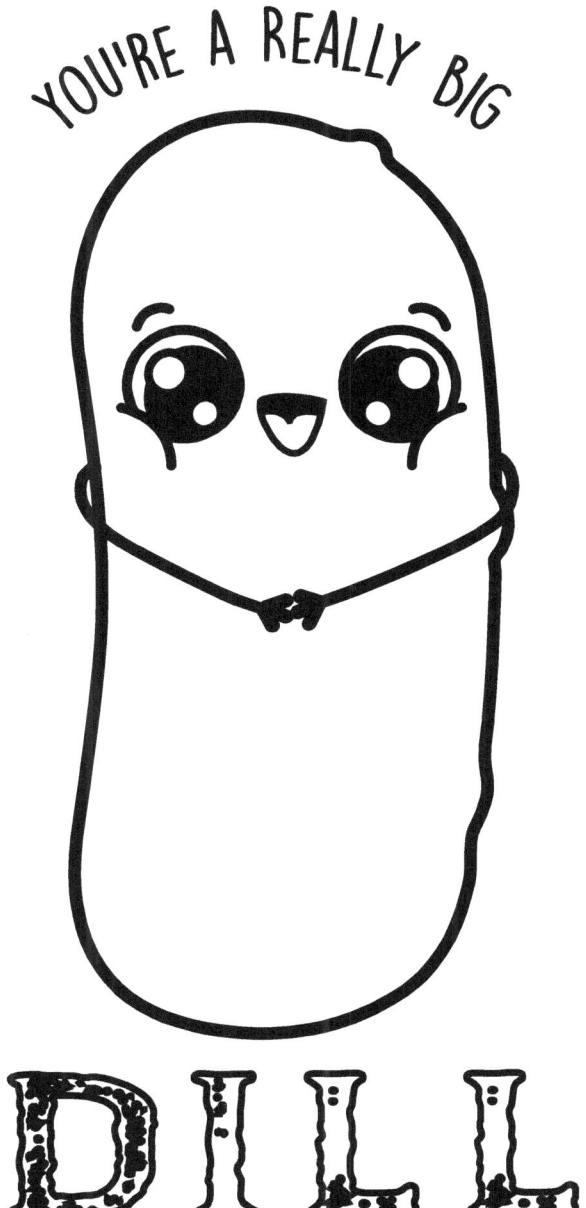

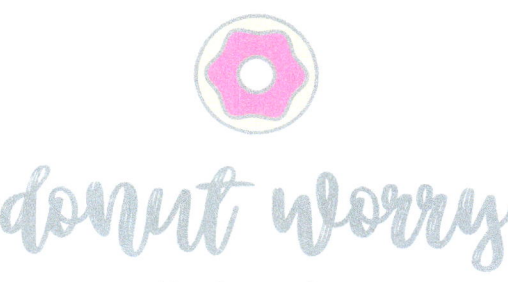

donut worry

THIS PAGE
INTENTIONALLY
LEFT BLANK
(FOR MARKER USERS)

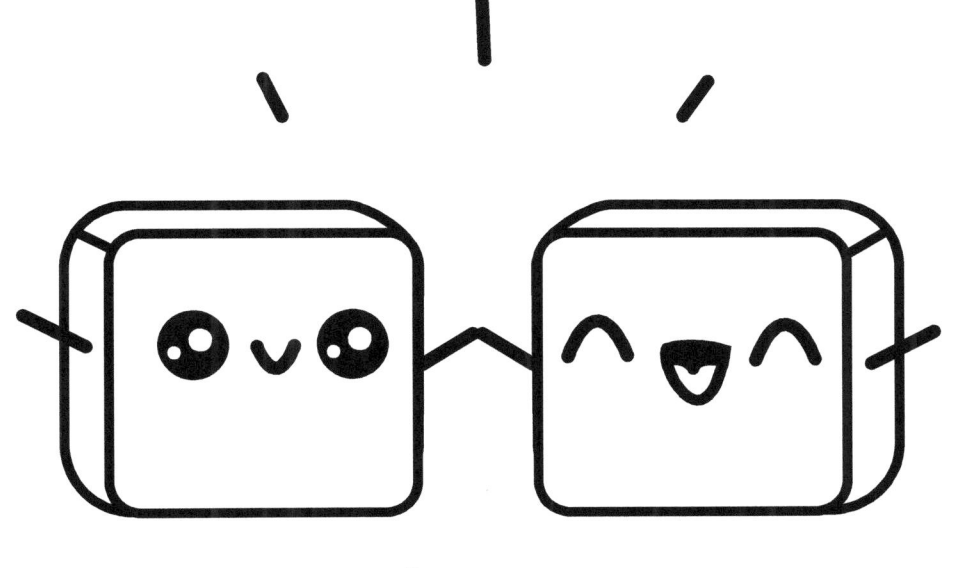

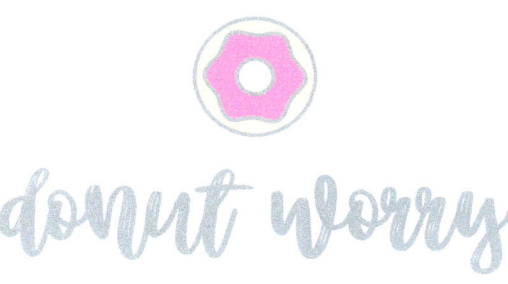

donut worry

THIS PAGE
INTENTIONALLY
LEFT BLANK
(FOR MARKER USERS)

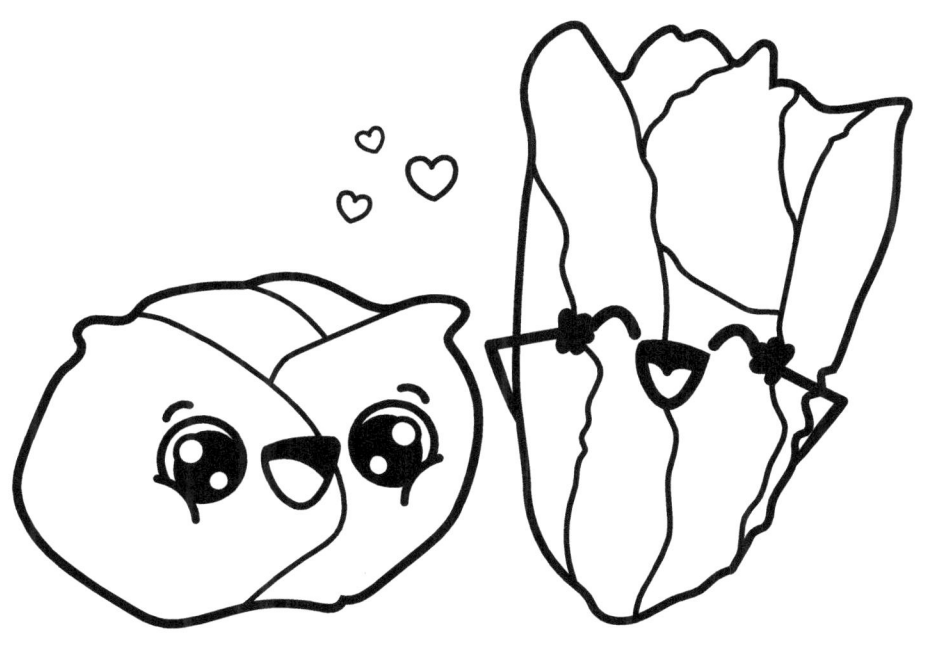

you're so
ROMAINE-TIC

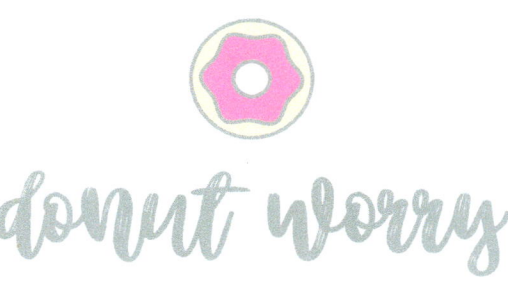

donut worry

THIS PAGE
INTENTIONALLY
LEFT BLANK
(FOR MARKER USERS)

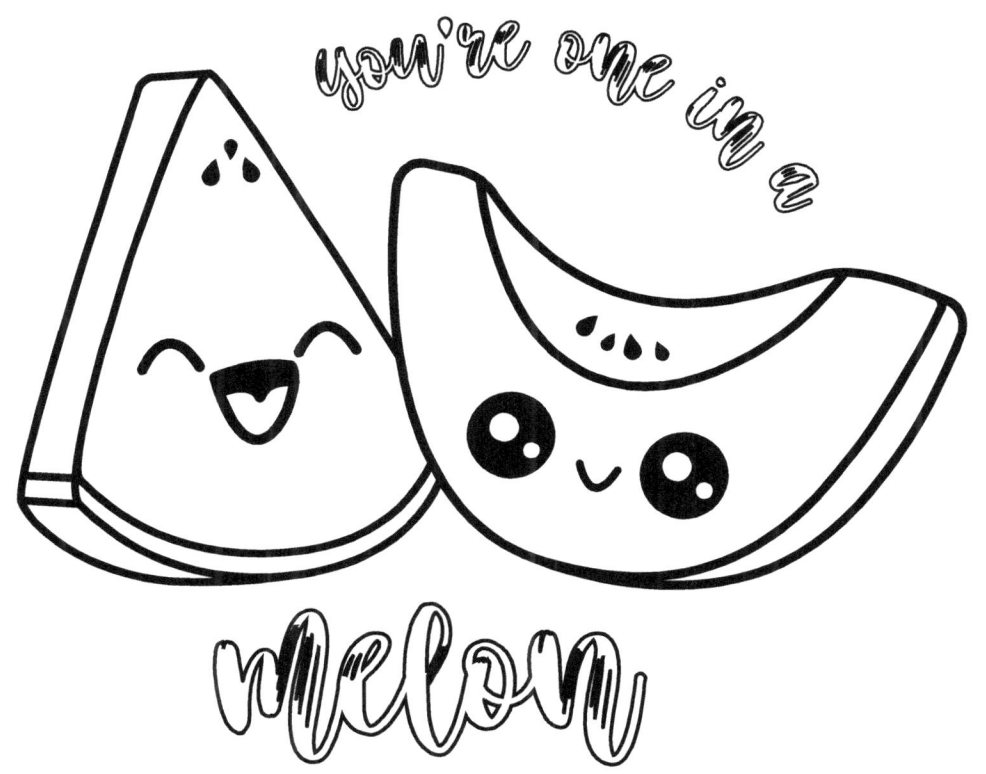

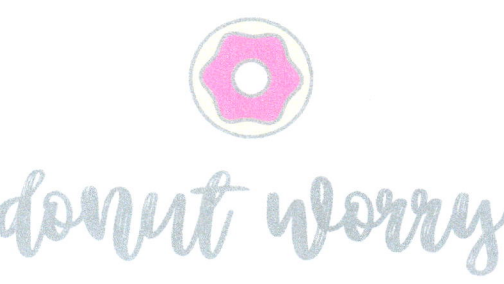

donut worry

THIS PAGE
INTENTIONALLY
LEFT BLANK
(FOR MARKER USERS)

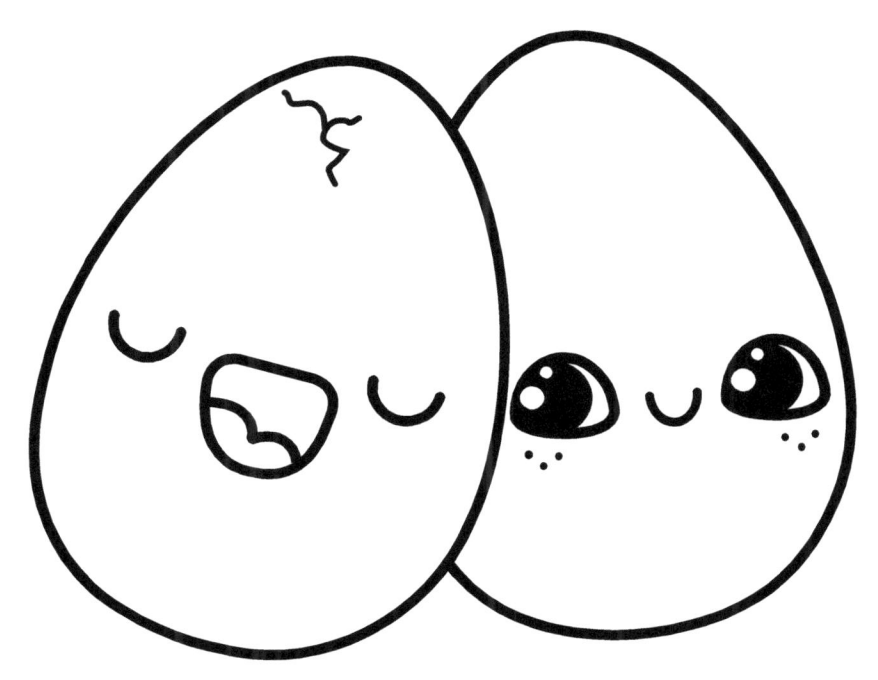

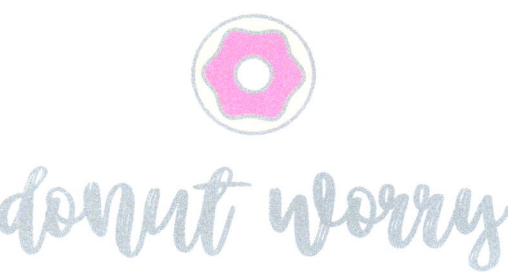

donut worry

THIS PAGE
INTENTIONALLY
LEFT BLANK
(FOR MARKER USERS)

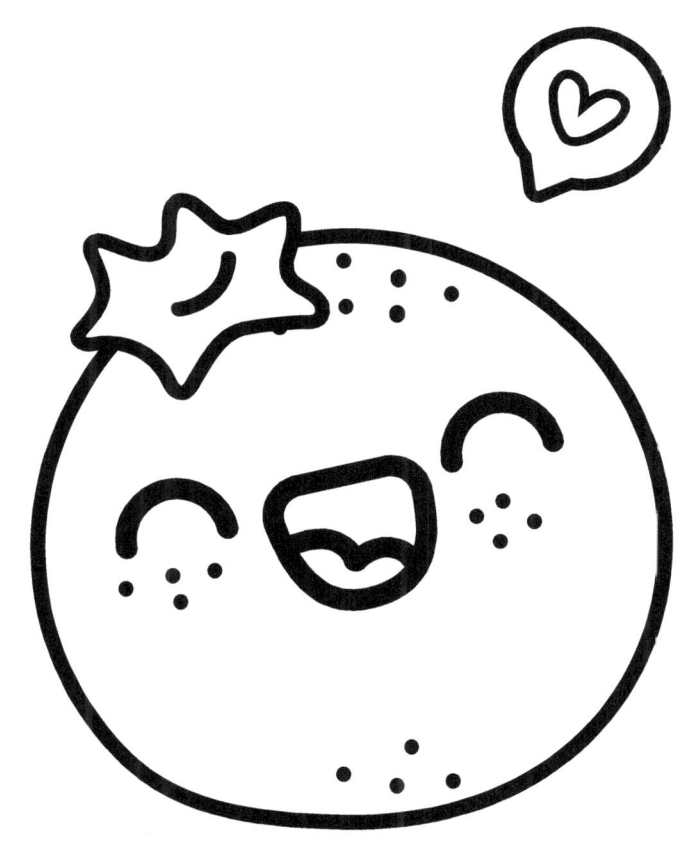

ORANGE YOU GLAD
you found this coloring book?

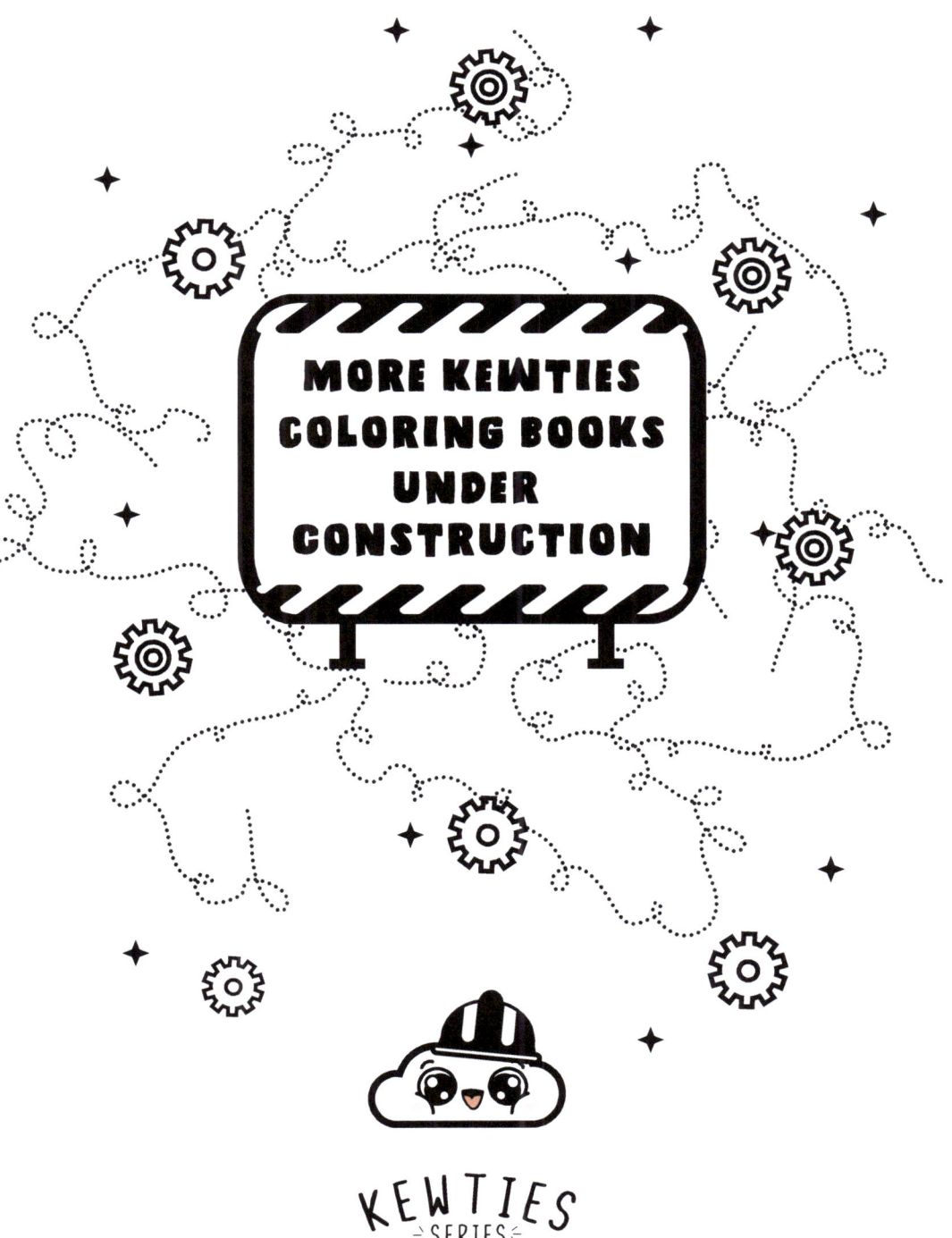

www.ingramcontent.com/pod-product-compliance
Lightning Source LLC
Chambersburg PA
CBHW040333220526
45473CB00009B/2674